YOUR KICKSTARTER IS ABOUT TO FAIL

AND WHAT YOU CAN DO ABOUT IT

By Carmelo G. Chimera

CHIMERA SOLUTIONS

The information contained herein is true and accurate to the best of the author's knowledge as of this writing. Any guarantees, or warranties for a particular use, are expressly denied. Nothing in this book is intended as legal advice.

CHIMERA SOLUTIONS

www.carmelochimera.com

ISBN: 978-0-9975776-0-0
ISBN-10:   0-9975776-0-6

First paperback printing: May 2016.

10 9 8 7 6 5 4 3 2 1

To my parents, Vince and Stacie.

Crowdfunding is about making dreams come true. But you can't expect the crowd to believe in you if you don't believe in yourself. And so a special thanks to my parents, who by believing in me taught me to believe in myself.

And thanks to that belief, all of my dreams feel possible.

CHAPTER 1

COME WITH ME IF YOU WANT TO BE FUNDED

So you've got a great idea. Maybe you're about to write the great American novel; maybe you're going to bring your short film to win the Crying Monkey Award at the Beijing Film Festival, or maybe you're ready to bring your kung fu robot bodyguard to market.

But how to secure the funding you need? Wait, you've got it - crowdfunding! Not just crowdfunding, but the biggest and best crowdfunding site around: Kickstarter. It's perfect! Free money will come to you in droves from the ether, and you'll be all taken care of. Now, to head over to Kickstarter where you'll create your account, start your project, and kick back while you get all the Internet money you need!

Hold it right there. If you press launch now, you're Kickstarter will fail! You won't get funded, and your brilliant product will never see the light of day. How do I know? Because I'm from the future. But that's good news! I didn't just come with warnings, I came with solutions.

It's not too late to avoid the most serious pitfalls facing crowdfunding hopefuls.

HOW TO USE THIS BOOK

If you're reading this, that means you want to know what the biggest challenges are facing crowdfunders and how you can avoid them. To be sure, this book will not tell you everything you need to know about running a successful campaign. There are tons of resources out there about a multitude of nuances and factors that play into a blockbuster Kickstarter campaign. (My book on the subject is coming soon, as of this writing!) Rather, this book is about a few major pitfalls that can spell disaster for your campaign.

It's *possible* to pay attention to everything in this book and still not have a successful campaign, let alone a five, six, or seven figure campaign. But it's nigh *impossible* to run a successful campaign if you ignore the landmines mapped out in this text.

This book is about avoiding certain failure, NOT about guaranteeing success.

WAIT, I'M ALREADY MID-CAMPAIGN, AND I THOUGHT THIS BOOK WOULD SAVE ME?

This book is designed to prepare you to avoid pitfalls *before* you launch your crowdfunding campaign. These principles are preventative. If you're mid-campaign, and you're afraid you aren't going to reach your funding goal, the principles in this book will not save your campaign.

But that does not mean all hope is lost. If your campaign may not get funded, you have two options:

1) Let the campaign finish and see what happens. If you don't get funded, you can always re-launch but this time with the principles herein on your side.

2) Cancel the campaign, and then relaunch with the principles of this book. Whether your campaign is successful or not, Kickstarter will archive it forever, and you'll always have an unfunded campaign on your profile. If you see that as a blemish, you can avoid it IF you cancel before the campaign funding deadline.

My strong advice is to go the second route. Cancel the campaign, regroup, then give it your all and remember everything we're about to talk about. If you want advice or coaching before your next campaign, or if you want to see if your current campaign is salvageable, you can always reach out to me. My contact information is at the end of this book, and I'm always happy to assist crowdfunding hopefuls.

WHAT'S ON THE AGENDA

Running a successful Kickstarter campaign takes planning, skill, creativity, and grit. There are tons of awesome Kickstarter projects live *right now* trying to attract backers. That's why if you've **never backed a Kickstarter campaign**, you probably don't understand - or at least, will have trouble conceptualizing - what makes a good campaign page. And, the Kickstarter community will think you're a "taker", and they'll know you're not a "giver" just by looking at your profile.

Once you do launch, your campaign is fighting the Internet's attention against hundreds of other Kickstarters, videos of cute cats, and Bob Ross memes. Your campaign could win that fight, but it's going to lose because **you haven't built an audience**. You need a crew of interested people who want what you're selling, and who are willing to go and spread the good word for you.

Whether you get funded or not, your project might fail if you haven't **prepared a budget**. Backers may not have faith in your project if you can't show that you've planned how to use their money, and even if you get funded your funds may not be enough if you haven't planned appropriately.

Surely, people will flock to your project, spreading the good word across the land until you're swimming in a pool of cash like Scrooge McDuck when they see how awesome your product is going to be! But they can't see the future, and they can't appreciate how great your product is because **your product is too incomplete** to show it off in all its glory.

"Ha ha!" you're thinking. "Nice try, but I already *got* funded! Thanks for nothing, sucker!" Wow, you're aggressive. But hold on, you eager mcbeaver. Your project isn't a success until your backers have received the rewards they were promised - and you're going to have an angry mob on your hands because you didn't **prepare for fulfillment** before you launched your campaign! And so we end where we began.

If you're ready to launch a hugely successful project, we'll end with a discussion of some resources and next steps to have an awesome campaign!

WHY SHOULD I LISTEN TO YOU ANYWAY?

"Wait a minute, tough guy," you're thinking. "Who are you and why should I give two Zack Snyder films about your opinion?" Great question. But I'll kindly remind you that you wanted this book, so simmer down.

I'm going to level with you: a year ago, I didn't know the first thing about crowdfunding. I graduated *summa cum laude* from Carthage College with a B.A. in philosophy before I attended the University of Chicago Law School. While in law school at the tender age of 21, I opened my first brick-and-mortar comic book store, Chimera's Comics, which is now a chain of three stores in the southwest suburbs of Chicago. I took a job at a mid-size law firm in Chicago, which I quit to open my own law practice and focus on my writing.

And all the while, I had a dream, just like yours. I had a product I believed in, and a project that I would do anything to see come to life. I wrote an original graphic novel called *Magnificent*, and for years, it had taken a backseat to my education and my stores. I needed a way to energize myself and my co-creator Steven Brown (who cofounded Chimera's Comics with me). We also needed funding to print the book in a format that would look proud next to other graphic novels, rather than something homemade.

After watching three creators I personally knew have awesome success with Kickstarter all within a few weeks of each other, I set about to launch my crowdfunding campaign. It may have been my time in law school, or my time running my businesses, or maybe even my time as an investigative reporter in college, but I knew I needed to scope things out before I dove headfirst into the deep end of crowdfunding without a life preserver.

I have a guiding philosophy in life: I don't gamble. I like to cheat. I only gamble when I can play with a stacked deck. So I set about stacking the deck to make sure my Kickstarter campaign would be a success. I knew I could do it - I knew I could become good enough to succeed, even if I wouldn't necessarily become a guru overnight. You see, I didn't know anything about business when I opened my first comic book store, but I spent *nine months* writing a 150-page business plan and teaching myself everything there was to know about running a physical retail store. I set about to do the same for Kickstarter.

For three months before I launched, and ever since, I immersed myself in research on crowdfunding. I read the books by leading experts, I listened to podcasts, I tore through blog posts. I even sought out the experts and asked them questions - remember, there's no substitute for human intelligence.

In the end, it worked. My first Kickstarter campaign was 133% funded, with an average pledge amount nearly triple the Kickstarter average. I'd beaten the odds in more ways than one, and as of this writing *Magnificent* is being prepped to send to our printers.

WHAT'S IN IT FOR ME

"But what do you get out of this, Carmelo?" Crowdfunding helped make one of my dreams come true. And every day I peruse Kickstarter, and I see awesome projects doing the same thing. I also see projects and pages from people who *clearly* haven't put in the time to organize a great campaign. I'm talking about projects with no backers at all, or projects with no campaign copy and a single 11-minute video, or projects with no updates or images. And I feel for these folks because I believe in people, and I can't assign these projects to laziness or stupidity. I believe these projects come from a *misunderstanding* of crowdfunding generally and of Kickstarter specifically. And I think, "if only they could hear me!" If only they could hear me, I might be able to help, and they might be able to see their dreams come true.

There's a more selfish reason too. A rising tide raises all ships. Crowdfunding is a social tool; by definition it requires a lot of people to work effectively. Every successful project - not just one that funds successfully, but fulfills its promises - further cements the legitimacy of the crowdfunding model.

And, every successful project brings new people, new backers, new eyes to crowdfunding. The first project a person backs is the hardest - even though signup is relatively easy, the time it takes to start an account and input payment information is a high enough opportunity cost to scare people away in our fast-paced, low-attention span world. But every subsequent pledge is just a matter of a single click. Good campaigns bring more users into Kickstarter, and that's good for everyone.

I also have a very unselfish reason for writing this book. As I mentioned, I did a lot of research to learn what I know about crowdfunding. That research came from the hard work of a lot of people. Not just the hard work associated with writing their books, or recording their podcasts. Not even the hard work from their own research. Rather, their knowledge came from running their own campaigns. From their hard-earned successes, and their hard-fought failures. These folks put themselves out there, and I need to do the same and give back what I've learned. I can't just be a taker. I need to be a giver. That's how crowdfunding works.

CHAPTER 2

YOU'VE NEVER BACKED A KICKSTARTER

You're getting ready to launch your Kickstarter. You love your project, and you know the world will too. So you have a Kickstarter account, click the link to start creating your campaign, and start typing away. You pick a title, a description, write your story, create some rewards, upload a picture, and click launch. Awesome! But, how do you know your campaign is any good? How do you know it even *looks* like a Kickstarter campaign? Let's assume your product is as awesome as you believe - I have faith in you. That does not mean your Kickstarter campaign remotely resembles what it should. And even if it does, your backers will see that you haven't backed any other projects - will they want to give to someone who doesn't give back?

DIRECT CORRELATION

John Coveyou, a crowdfunder and blogger at Genius Games, has researched Kickstarter statistics in depth and found a direct correlation between a project's likelihood of success and the number of projects its creator has backed. Coveyou told Richard Bliss, crowdfunding guru and host of the podcast "Funding the Dream", that:

> "It is incredibly clear that the number of projects a [ ] project creator has backed, that amount increases at almost the same rate as the success rates increase. So if a project creator has backed 1-5 projects, it's right around a 27% success rate. 6-10 projects backed, it jumps up to 48%. 11-25 projects it jumps up to 52%, 26-50 projects back jumps up to 64%…100-200 projects backed, it jumps up to 72%."[1]

Should you go out right now and back 100 different Kickstarter projects to increase your odds? Well, maybe, but correlation does not confirm causation. As Mark Twain said, "there are lies, damned lies, and statistics." So before you jump the gun with this knowledge, we need to think about why this data might be so. Only then can you turn it to your advantage.

---

[1] Coveyou, John. "6 Stats to Kickstarter Success." Interview. Funding The Dream. Bliss, Richard. 26 Oct. 2014. Web. <https://www.buzzsprout.com/4646/215212-6-stats-to-kickstarter-success-ep-230-w-john-coveyou>.

So why might the number of projects you back correlate to your likelihood of success? As near as I can tell, there are two ways: first, a person who backs more projects is more familiar with the platform and in what makes a project stand out. How will you know what your project should look like if you've never seen one before, let alone a good one? The second cause, as I see it, is being a good member of the community. Crowdfunding is about give and take, and if everyone can see you're only a taker, people may have a problem giving to you.

WHAT'S IT SUPPOSED TO LOOK LIKE?

If you're having a hard time understanding this point, let's look at an analogy. Let's say you're trying to draw a picture of the Taj Mahal. (This assumes of course that you can draw, and that you know what the Taj Mahal is. Just roll with me here.) Do you know what the Taj Mahal looks like? When was the last time you looked at a picture of it? Even if you remember what it looks like, how accurate do you think your drawing is going to be if the last time you looked at it was during your high school world history class?

Here's another analogy. Let's say you're trying to bake a chocolate cake. But you don't have a recipe, and you've never eaten chocolate cake. Even if you come up with the right ingredients and bake it for the right time, when you're done how will you know the thing you pulled out of the oven is a chocolate cake? How will you know it tastes right if you don't know what it's supposed to taste like?

You might be happy with your chocolate cake, but will the people you baked it for like the cake? Will they even try to eat your cake if they know you've never baked or even eaten chocolate cake before?

So it is with Kickstarter campaigns. To be successful, your campaign needs a certain quality to it, and your potential backers won't have confidence in you if they can see you haven't even backed another project.

You might say, "Carmelo, Kickstarter takes me step by step through the components of creating the campaign. It's not rocket science." Well, you're right that anyone could fill out a Kickstarter. Not anyone can make a good one. Let's take a quick look at the elements of your campaign page and knock down a few misconceptions so you don't hurt yourself.

When creating a project, Kickstarter asks for a number of elements, but I'm going to go through a few main ones to show you that there's more than meets the eye, and you'll need to physically browse Kickstarter to truly understand these elements. The major elements you cannot take for granted are the image, the title, the short blurb, the story, and the video.

Image

The first thing Kickstarter asks for isn't even the name of your project, it's the image. This is the first thing people see of your campaign - and if it sucks, it'll be the last thing they see.

The image shows up when people are scrolling through projects. It's also the image that will display in previews when you share the project on social media sites, and if you're lucky enough to get any news coverage, it'll be the image that the press pulls unless you provide a different one.

"I have an Instagram account, Carmelo," you're saying. "I know how to put a picture online."

But it's not that simple. Do you know what resolution your photo is supposed to be, or what aspect ratio? How will your image look on a desktop? How about on a phone, where most people browse the Internet now? Does your image look good small? Is your image oriented in landscape or portrait?

Beyond these components, here's a question that can only be answered if you look around Kickstarter a bit: will your image stand out?

Browse through some Kickstarter projects in the same category you're in. Which projects jump out at you? Once you determine that, think about what about their project image speaks to you. Is it minimalist? Is it text-heavy? Is it colorful?

There's a lot more to this than just uploading a picture. And the only way to find out if your picture is any good is to look at other Kickstarter project images. When you select your image, **do**:

- Look at other images to see what stands out to you
- Make your image the correct aspect ratio (16:9)

- Make your image look good on a small screen
- Make your image accurately represent your project (no click bait!)

And when you've done all that, **do not:**

- Crop a different image so it fits into Kickstarter
- Put a lot of text onto your image
- Show something inaccurate to your project
- Upload an image with too low resolution

Title

Your project needs a title, and you only have 60 characters to do it. There are one of two big mistakes you could make here: the first is making your title too long. The second is making your title too short.

Even though you get 60 characters, your title will get cut off in the search or browse functions of Kickstarter if it's too long. That means any essential information needs to be succinct, and front-loaded (in other words, toward the beginning of the title). It should also be truncated so that someone can get the whole title at a glance. Your potential backers have a lot of projects to browse through, and if they can't digest your title and get interested *quick*, they may just move on.

On the other hand, it can be too short. The title will be indexed in Kickstarter's search feature - which means that if you want a stranger to stumble on the project (or even a friend looking to back you), you MUST include any key words that you think describe your project!

There's a little tension here - because I do not think the title is the place to start describing your work. Save that for the blurb. However, you do want your project to show up in search terms. And, you project title might be meaningless without a little description. For example, my first project was called "Magnificent." That was probably a bad title - I should have put "Magnificent: An Original Graphic Novel" or something to that effect because, without that descriptor, the word "magnificent" is meaningless. Since it was my first time, the brand didn't have any power behind it either.

Short Blurb

The short blurb is only 135 characters. This is where I really start to get worried about you folks. I've seen a lot of bad blurbs, but to list them here would require another book, and "ain't nobody got time for that."

There are three archetypal *bad* blurbs I forbid you from using. I have seen blurbs start off with "Hi my name is" and that's wrong. I've seen blurbs start to tell your personal story, and that's wrong too. I've also seen blurbs ask for support. "Help me, back my project, I need your help." *Of course you do.* That's WHY you're on Kickstarter!

The blurb needs to be a short, accurate, attention-grabbing slogan that describes your product. Don't waste any words on the kinds of blurbs I just described. Think of a product slogan. What would grab someone's attention? Even if it's abstract, so long as it conveys *the feeling* of your product to the potential backer, that's a good blurb.

Think of the catchphrases on the commercials and products you use every day. Or the taglines you see on movie posters. Or the slogans on billboards. These are great short blurbs that you could emulate.

Story

The story is the meat of your project. This is your chance to describe your product in detail and explain why it's awesome. But I've read too many stories that miss the point or are simply unreadable.

Kickstarter is NOT GoFundMe. This is not the place to write a letter like, "Hi I'm Carmelo, and I really want to make my comic book so please pledge to my project because I need money to make my comic, thanks. XOXO, Carmelo." If you write a letter like that, I will find you, and I will feed you a print copy of this book in your hands. GoFundMe is a site with less structure or restrictions, and a great place for personal "help me" projects like "My dog got hit by a car and needs surgery."

I think GoFundMe is great because I love seeing a community come together to help someone in need, but it's not Kickstarter. With GoFundMe projects, backers expect a lot less back - if anything at all. But Kickstarter projects thrive when they have a level of professionalism because the backers also want something in return (probably your product). So your story can NOT just be an appeal for help.

It MUST explain why the backer needs your product, and demonstrate that you have the ability to take money and use it well to make your project real.

Your story has to explain a couple of things: what your product is, why your product is awesome, what you're going to use your backer's money for, and how you plan to bring your product to life.

But it has to be readable. Think about articles you like online. What's popular? They have photos, they have titles and subtitles, they have lists. When was the last time you got a link to an article online that was 800 words of uninterrupted text in a single paragraph? And if you got such a link, did you read it? If you did, you're a better human being than I am.

When you write your story, **do:**

- Make it as visual as possible by using lots of pictures, graphics, etc.
- Break up the text into paragraphs and give the paragraphs headings and subheadings
- Explain what sets your product apart
- Address how you plan to use your backer's hard earned money

And when you're done with all that, **do not:**

- Write a letter asking for help
- Talk only about yourself rather than your product
- Make any typos or use any bad grammar

The Video

The last thing you cannot take for granted is your project video. We could write a book on just this topic, but today all I care about is that you not take this for granted. I see tons of projects launch without a video. I recall one project with almost no description and only its 11-minute video to convey information.

Your video should be awesome because for most people this is all they'll see on your page and they won't even bother to read your story. But it doesn't need to be fancy, or expensive. Do *not* skip the video because it's hard, or because you can't afford it. You can make an inexpensive (read: free) video on your own laptop with a webcam, or even hire someone for a reasonable price on a website like UpWork or Fiverr.

It's *not* that hard to make a video. It does not need fancy graphics, or fancy music, or animation. It would be great if it did, and if you plan to make a 6-figure project you might consider investing in this. But just because you can't make an expensive looking video does not mean you shouldn't make one.

If you go the webcam route, don't drone on endlessly. Think about the videos you watch online. Will you watch a video someone sends you if it's 5 minutes long? 8 minutes? 12? If you start, will you even finish it? Brevity is the name of the game with your video, ideally under 2 minutes long.

How will you cram all the information into 2 minutes? That's what your story is for. The video is NOT the place for details you expect the backers to remember. It's not the place to go through your rewards, or dates, or figures. This is the place to convey the passion about your product. If it's a practical product, this is the place to show it in action.

Use the video to set the tone for your project. Don't take this for granted!

TAKE A PENNY, LEAVE A PENNY

On Kickstarter, backers will be able to see your profile showing which projects you've created (if any) and which projects you've backed. Even if they don't look at your profile, Kickstarter will include directly under your name the number of projects you've backed.

If you've never backed a project, all of your backers will see that. Believe it or not, the number of projects you've backed *directly correlates* to your odds of success. In other words, the more projects a creator has backed, the higher the probability their own project will get funded.

One explanation for this phenomenon might be the things we discussed above. But another explanation is, without backing a project you look like a taker, not a giver. Kickstarter is a community, which means it thrives on the give and the take. You can't just take and take without giving something in return. People will know that's what you've done, and it will reflect poorly on your reputation. It will look like you don't really care about crowdfunding, but that you showed up to get a quick payday.

"But Carmelo, I'm not made of money." Well, I didn't say you had to personally fund a half dozen projects! Pledge a couple of bucks, whatever you can spare. Who knows, maybe as you browse you'll find a project that really excites you or a product that you really want! While I was doing research for this book, I saw a project called Quik'Stix that got me super jazzed - a reusable, super sticky gel-pad I can use to hold items or electronics in place. I plan to stick my remote controls to my bedside table.

So get out there and back a few projects!

YOUR ASSIGNMENT FOR THE DAY, CLASS

This section of the book is NOT meant to be a step-by-step guide to creating your project on Kickstarter. This is designed to help you see that you shouldn't just dive headfirst into the deep end until you've put your toes in the water first. There's a lot more to a great campaign than meets the eye, and when it comes to the essential elements like your image, title, short blurb, story, and video, if you take them for granted your project WILL fail.

But the moral of this story is, go to Kickstarter! Go there now! Look at some projects, browse around, and read the stories! Watch the videos. The whole *point* of this chapter is that there's some information you can't get unless you actually look at Kickstarter. And if I write another 100 pages, it's *still* not a substitute for looking at Kickstarter.

And don't just look - find something awesome and pledge! You'll get project updates, you'll get to communicate with the creator (lower case c), and you'll get some insight into the backer experience so you can make sure YOUR backers have a great experience.

But backing a project isn't just about education. It's about being a good Kickstarter citizen.

CHAPTER 3

YOU DON'T HAVE AN AUDIENCE

Did you check out some Kickstarters and back a few? If you didn't, I'll wait. Go on. Do it now.

…

All done? Good. You're getting ready to launch your project, but do you have anyone to launch it to? You can have the biggest launch in the world - fireworks and all - but if you haven't invited anyone to the party, your launch will end not with a bang, but a whimper.

A common Kickstarter misconception is that you make a campaign, and then start telling people about it. Wrong. *Your campaign has succeeded - or failed - before you press launch*. The idea that "if you build it, they will come" does NOT apply to Kickstarter campaigns.

Having an audience is NOT just about the money. An audience is THE best form of marketing you can hope for. There is absolutely no substitute for face-to-face, word-of-mouth advertising based on genuine relationships between people. Everything from television commercials to bus-shelter posters is all an attempt to connect with people precisely because it's impossible to talk face-to-face to every possible consumer. Advertising is the next best thing.

But you have the ability to communicate directly with a network, and they can communicate with their respective networks, and pretty soon you have a campaign.

Word of mouth can NOT be understated. Take a look at *Magnificent* again. Of the 125 people who backed Steven and my project, approximately 1/3 of these were either our friends and family, or friends of our friends and family. 1/3 of these were customers of Chimera's Comics, and only 1/3 were strangers who discovered the project through marketing efforts.

That means up to 2/3 of our support came from an audience we'd established *before* we launched.

YOU ALREADY HAVE AN AUDIENCE

What you may not realize is that you probably already have an audience - you just haven't identified that audience and planned on contacting them. As John Donne wrote, "No man is an island."

Do you have family? Friends? These people may help you. You may be reluctant to ask them for help - a lot of people are. But you'll need to get passed that because crowdfunding is all about asking people for money. Remember that you aren't begging - and I discourage you from doing so - because you're offering rewards. You are offering value in return for their support.

You may need more than just those folks to get funded. Are you in a book club? A youth church group? An entrepreneurs networking group? Do you have co-workers? Any and all of these people are critical to your success.

The question really is, are they interested in what you're selling? If you're trying to crowdfund a children's book, you can probably count on co-workers with kids to back you. If you're trying to crowdfund a new drone/coffee-maker hybrid, your friends who still use typewriters and rotary phone probably aren't going to be interested.

All of these people are your primary base. But will it be enough?

GROWING YOUR AUDIENCE

Take a look at your funding goal (we'll look closer at this in the next chapter). Let's say, for argument's sake, that your goal is small - say $1,000. The average Kickstarter campaign pledge is $25.[2] So let's divide your goal ($1,000) by the average pledge ($25). That means we need 40 people to back your project if you are to be successful.

Do you know 40 people interested in the product you want to produce? Do you have 40 close friends or family members you can count on to support your project? If so you're in great shape. If not, you need to grow the audience

[2] "Building Rewards." Kickstarter. Web. <https://www.kickstarter.com/help/handbook/rewards>.

before you can expect to be successful. 40 doesn't sound so bad. But if you're trying to raise $10,000 - now you need 400 backers. Sounds a lot harder now.

You CAN find some of those backers after you launch. In fact, you will find some. But the more you can count on before you launch, the better your chances. And even if you think you can reach 400 people, will each and every single one of them back the project? You probably need to reach many, many times that number to get 400 backers.

So how do you grow your audience? This could be (and probably is) a book all unto itself. But with crowdfunding there are a couple of things that jump out at me:

- **Back projects** - increase your profile in the crowdfunding community by backing other projects. Even if those creators don't turn around and back you, other backers will see that you're one of them (see the previous chapter);
- **Reach out on social media** - Facebook, Twitter, and Instagram allow you to have the face-to-face, word-of-mouth interaction we talked about with billions of people around the globe, not just the few dozen people you see in person every day;
- **Paid advertising -** If you're willing to pay for it, the Internet can give you a lot of bang for your buck with micro-targeted advertising directly to folks who are likely to want what you're trying to sell;

- **Create free content** - By putting out free/low-cost but valuable content into the world of the type you want to sell, you can build an audience of interested leads. Blogs, podcasts, and free eBooks or a way to do this. Yes, that's the idea with this book too which I say proudly because it's no trick - you aren't beholden to my future project just because you accepted this one.

FINDING YOUR AUDIENCE V. CREATING YOUR AUDIENCE

There is an important philosophical decision you have to make early on when growing an audience: do you want to find an audience for your product, OR do you want to find a product for an audience? The difference between these two philosophies can completely transform your strategy.

Is your goal to create a specific product, or is your goal to make money? There's nothing wrong with making money - I don't mean that condescendingly. But your goal determines whether or not you're looking for an audience or a product.

Let's say you have a product that you're very excited about - a documentary you want to film, or a traveling art display. You're passionate about it, you care about it, you want it to come to life, and that's why you've turned to crowdfunding. That's spectacular - but that means you have a product, and you need to find an audience. To do that, you'll need to identify *similar* products and find out who is spending money on those products? That's your target audience. And when you've identified your target audience, it's a matter of communicating with that target.

But let's say you just want to make money. Well, rather than take a product and then *look* for an audience, you can find the audience first and then figure out what they need. If you can identify a need for an audience, you don't have to hope someone wants your product - you can tailor the product to fill that need. This is even easier than you think if the audience you select is one you yourself are a part of. In his classic book *The 4-Hour Workweek*, entrepreneur Timothy Ferris writes at length about this idea. He explains that you should think about a product you yourself might need or use. Then, think about who else would have that need.

Let's say you're a lawyer who wants to drum up a new business, and you think a website is the way to do it. An hour-long video or an eBook on web design specifically for lawyers would be enormously helpful - either because you want to make it yourself, or so you can make informed decisions about the design of a site someone else is building for you. Well, if you think other lawyers would want that too then you have found a product for an existing audience. If you're confident that you are representative of other lawyers, then you don't need to wonder if there's someone out there who wants your product - you already know that there is, and you know who they are.

Ferris' point of view is very attractive, and it might be (probably is) more lucrative.

MEET THEM WHERE THEY'RE AT

Once you know what your audience is - whether you found the audience, or started with the audience - you need to communicate your message to them. Whether you choose to do so through word-of-mouth, or through paid advertising, in order to communicate with your audience you have to meet them where they're at. In fundraising generally it's called engagement.

A former colleague of mine, David Gonzalez, taught this concept to me when consulting at my comic book store. As of this writing, David is the Executive Director of The Port Ministries, a non-profit in the Back Of The Yards community in Chicago that provides health care, education, food, and faith ministry to one of the city's poorest and most dangerous communities. David used to run a non-profit in the Glencoe School District, and before that ran a charity in Rhode Island that used art and music to help at-risk youth. So this is a man with a lot of experience fundraising, and the same principles apply.

David explained this concept to me literally and metaphorically. Literally, you need to find your audience. Who are they? Where do they hang out? What websites do they visit? Find them, talk to them there.

Metaphorically, where is your audience at mentally? What do they value? What matters to them? What language do they respond to? What would motivate them to help you?

This is crucial both toward spreading your message and crafting your message to make sure it's effective. Let's take a look at *Magnificent* again. As you'll recall, 1/3 of the supporters were customers of Chimera's Comics. I drew my target audience to me - broadly, people who are interested in graphic novels. I established lines of communication with them - I'd built 3 Facebook pages, a Twitter account, and an e-mail list with these people. And I physically gathered them into three physical places (my stores).

So I had found interested parties, formed a genuine relationship with them, and had a way to communicate with them. And without those 40 or so backers, *Magnificent* would NOT have happened. I knew what those folks wanted based on their shopping preferences - so I knew they'd be interested in a cool graphic novel and my communication to them focused on that score.

With friends or family, the motivation is different. They'll want to help because it matters to you, so to them your message has to be about passion, about why this project is important to you, about what their support means to you.

Whatever your audience is, understanding where they are and what they want is essential to monetizing their support.

CHAPTER 4

YOU DIDN'T MAKE A BUDGET

You've looked at a few Kickstarter and built some street cred by backing a few projects. You've used that knowledge to design an eye-catching image, title, short blurb, and story. You've started building the buzz about your project, and you're ready to find interested customers to become your backers.

You want to finish designing your campaign, but then you hit an important question. It seems so obvious because it's why you're here, but you pause because you haven't thought it through: how much money are you trying to raise?

Seems like a simple question. Just type in any number, and the pledges will roll in until you're lighting your cigars with burned up copies of *Action Comics* #1 like Krusty the Clown.

But you've a lot to consider. Your goal is *not* the net amount (meaning, after expenses/costs/fees) of money you're going to receive, and it's going to have to be enough to create your product AND get all of your backers their rewards. But you can't compensate for this by just asking for more money - you have to figure out if the amount of money you're looking for is even feasible, given your project and audience. A high goal isn't a problem - unless it's out of touch with your resources and intended market.

If you ask for too much, you may not get funded, and if you get funded your project will fail if you haven't asked for enough.

BUDGETS ARE ABOUT MORE THAN NUMBERS

I hate math. I'm sure you do too. If you love math, I probably don't trust you. That doesn't mean we can't be friends, of course, I just question your goals as a human being.

The budget sounds intimidating to someone who isn't comfortable with numbers. But your budget is about more - it's about what your goals are as a creator. If you're just looking for quick cash, I'm not sure crowdfunding is the best way to do that. It's certainly not the easiest. So you need to assess your project and think about what you want.

Do you need money to produce your product, start to finish? Will it require a prototype? If it's a performance or a film, do you have to cover salaries for others or even yourself to give you time to work on the product?

Or maybe your product is complete. Maybe it's a print on demand book or a work of art you've already completed. Maybe you need crowdfunding to market and distribute your product.

Maybe you need enough money to take your idea from a sketch on the back of a cocktail napkin all the way to best seller.

You HAVE to think about these things before you launch your project, and that's what your budget is designed to help you do. If you only need marketing and distribution funds for your completed product, your goal can be much lower. If you need to create your product soup-to-nuts, you're going to need much more. The lower your goal, the better your odds of getting funded.

Through my research, I have found as of yet not statistically significant correlation between the amount of a project's goal and the final amount a project raises. So what I'm saying is, if your product is awesome and you've effectively communicated with your audience, it doesn't matter what you started asking for. Your project can go gangbusters. But better to hit your goal, and see how *overfunded* you can be, then to struggle and hit your initial goal.

Your budget will force you to think through things you would not otherwise have considered. And your budget is as important to your audience as it is to you.

INSPIRING CONFIDENCE

Did you know 9% of Kickstarter projects that ARE successfully funded STILL fail because they fall through during the fulfillment phase?[3] We'll get to that later in the chapter where I chastise you for not planning for fulfillment, but it's relevant here too.

Kickstarter is fond of saying that it's NOT a store, that the backers are investing their money and support into a creator in the hopes their project comes to life - there are no guarantees. So from the backer perspective, there's a good chance that even if they do give you money, you might screw it up and leave them with nothing.

Creating a budget and *showing that budget* to your potential backers is a way to inspire confidence. It's a way of saying, "I didn't pull this number out of my butt, I thought it through and here is how I'm going to use that money."

There are some folks who are super-fans and will back you regardless. But to those on the fence or those who are total strangers, what reason do they have to trust you? Particularly if this is your first attempt at crowdfunding?

Make a budget, and show it off.

THINGS TO CONSIDER

When making your budget, there's a couple of major expenses you're going to have to be sure you've covered:

---

[3] Mollick, Ethan R., "Delivery Rates on Kickstarter". December 4, 2015. http://ssrn.com/abstract=2699251

- **Pre-Production**: Your product might require design work, development, or a prototype beforehand
- **Production:** Get multiple quotes on the production of your product to get the best bang for your (and your backer's) bucks
- **Marketing**: Won't you need money to sell your product? What's more, what about money to advertise your Kickstarter?
- **Postage/Shipping**: This WILL kill your project and so it gets its own chapter later
- **Fees**: Don't forget that whatever you raise, you'll lose about 10% right off the top for fees to Kickstarter, for credit card processing, and from backer attrition

THE TAX MAN COMETH

Another important factor you need to consider in advance is income taxes. In short, YES - your Kickstarter funds ARE taxable income (in the United States at least, I can't speak to other countries). If you don't reserve funds for this come tax season, you'll need to shell out of pocket, probably to the tune of one third of your Kickstarter funds. But I bring it up here instead of above because with proper budgeting, you may not have to pay any such tax.

Hold your horses, I'm not suggesting anything illegal. What I'm saying is, your Kickstarter project will definitely have a number of legitimate business expenses associated with it - production costs, design costs, independent contractors, advertising, etc. These costs are legitimately deducted from your income. Put another way, *if you spend most or all of the Kickstarter money on legitimate business expenses, there won't be any Kickstarter income left to pay taxes on.*

What does budgeting have to do with this? Well, if you ask for some arbitrary amount like $10,000 - but you only really need $4,000 - you'll end up paying taxes on the remaining $6,000 (leaving you with a SUPER ROUGH ESTIMATE of $2,000 in tax liability). So it's important to figure out what you're going to use the funds for before asking for them. Because if it's funds you plan to put into your pocket, you better set 1/3 aside for the tax man so you don't have to find it later.

SCALING UP

You'd love to be 100% funded - but wouldn't you rather be 200% funded? How about 1,000% funded? Who wouldn't - it's a crowdfunder's dream for their project to go viral and explode like that.

But what if your project isn't scalable? What if you get *too many backers*? How can that possibly happen? One example involves shipping. Your Kickstarter goal INCLUDES funds that you will use to ship rewards to your backers. This is a non-negligible expense. And their pledge had better be enough to cover the cost of the respective reward, as well as the cost of shipping those rewards. But shipping costs vary wildly between domestic and

International shipping. What if you get an over abundance of international backers?

Another example is in stretch goals. These are a common tactic to encourage backers to fund and promote your project even after you reach your goal by promising additional incentives or upgrades to your project. But those goals aren't free, and your new goal had better be enough to cover the stretch rewards you promised. For instance, in the *Magnificent* campaign, we promised every back hardcovers if we'd raised $10,000 (we didn't hit our goal, but we ended up paying out of pocket to do hardcovers anyway as a thank you to our backers). Hardcovers cost DOUBLE what paperbacks would have cost (especially when you account for the increased weight, increasing overseas freight costs). If $10,000 wasn't enough to cover the hardcovers, and if we hit that goal and committed to that upgrade, we could have been stuck between a rock and a hard place (see what I did there?).

As you budget, you have to make sure that your project will still be feasible at higher levels. And part of that comes from smart rewards planning.

REWARDING YOUR WALLET

Planning out your rewards and planning out your budget go hand-in-hand. Your rewards must provide enough value so a backer feels it's worth their money, but not so much value that you *lose* money when you pick up a backer.

The pledge level cannot be out of whack with the rewards you're offering. For example, let's say your project is to make a physical hardcopy of a comic book. Suggested retail price (SRP) on a 22-page comic book (most have 10 pages of ads I'm not counting) is approximately $3.99.

If the lowest pledge level to get a physical copy of the comic is $10, there's a serious problem, because I wouldn't pay that much for the comic book under any other situation. What's more, you'll probably sell the book for $3.99 to fans after you pay to print it, giving future customers a better deal than the backers who brought your project to life.

At the same time, the reward can't cost you so much to produce that you *lose* money when someone makes the pledge. Let's say you want to offer a t-shirt as a reward. If you're not printing in large quantities, a custom t-shirt could cost a pretty penny, depending on the style and type of printing. If it's screen printing, the process is only viable at large quantities and gets more expensive with every single color. So you use direct-to-garment or heat transfer, which costs you in the neighborhood of $10 a shirt. Well, to be worth it the pledge required had better be at least $20 so you make a worthwhile profit - and that's just for the shirt.

This is where we return to the budget. When you budget how much you need for your project, you have to consider how much it will cost you to fulfill each reward, and be sure that it's priced into your goals. If your rewards require you to create a bunch of expensive extra inventory, then your project goal may not be enough to make all of your backers happy.

If you don't take this problem seriously, let's look at one of the great Kickstarter disasters of all time, *Coolest Cooler: 21st Century Cooler that's Actually Cooler*.[4] The Coolest Cooler promised quite the spectacular creation - this cooler would include a rechargeable blender, a removable waterproof Bluetooth speaker, a USB charger, and more. At the time, the project was the highest funded Kickstarter project, raising $13 million in August 2014. As of this writing, most backers STILL don't have their rewards.

Why? According to Crowdfund Insider, despite raising $13 million the campaign only netted $7.4 million, which wasn't enough to fulfill the promised rewards.[5] Further, the creators saw this coming: in an e-mail to backers, project creator Ryan Grepper stated, "We knew that the Kickstarter funds, in the end, would not cover the actual cost of fulfilling all the backer orders."[6]

But wait, there's more. Grepper has *also* stated that the price point for the coolers was always too low to be feasible. The cooler is currently available for sale (and *in*

[4] https://www.kickstarter.com/projects/ryangrepper/coolest-cooler-21st-century-cooler-thats-actually/description

[5] Alois, JD. "Coolest Cooler Not So Cool as Project Runs Short of Cash - Crowdfund Insider." Crowdfund Insider. 27 Feb. 2016. http://www.crowdfundinsider.com/2016/02/82285-coolest-cooler-not-so-cool-as-project-runs-short-of-cash/

[6] Ibid.

stock, even while backers are waiting for their coolers) - on Amazon for $399.99, but backers were promised their coolers during the campaign for pledges as low as $165.[7]

This all sounds pretty frightening, but if I haven't put the fear of God into you yet, remember that frustrated backers have even gone so far as *physically threatening* the creators of the Coolest Cooler.[8]

So pretty please, with sugar on top, make a budget!

---

[7] Koebler, Jason. "Kickstarter's Biggest Shitshow Somehow Got Even Messier." Motherboard. 13 Apr. 2016. Web. http://motherboard.vice.com/read/a-very-uncool-cooler

[8] Ibid.

CHAPTER 5

YOUR PRODUCT IS TOO INCOMPLETE

By now you're probably anxious to launch your project. Your itchy trigger finger is hovering over your mouse, the cursor floating over the launch button. But don't touch that dial, because if you want your Kickstarter project to be successful, you have to have enough of your product complete to show everyone how cool it is.

Maybe you're saying, "Carmelo, my product is done. I'm ready to go." Well, then by all means, launch away. You can skip this lesson.

Maybe you're saying, "Carmelo, the whole reason I went to Kickstarter is to *create* my product. I don't have a partial project, much less a completed one." Then strap in, because this one's for you, you lucky so-and-so.

A Magnificent Failure

At first, I honestly wasn't sure this topic was worth its own chapter. But I have strong feelings about this because this is DEFINITELY an area where my Kickstarter failed big-time.

It's not easy to call the *Magnificent* Kickstarter a failure. Even though it was our first campaign we were overfunded, we hit stretch goals, and our average pledge was triple the Kickstarter average. But I know we would have made raised more if our project had been complete. When I launched the project, I had a completed script, pencilled artwork for a little more than half the graphic novel, and I could count the number of inked pages on a single hand. I did not have a single 100% completed page of the comic, let alone a page that was even in color. I had two promotional images designed as covers that were colored by a friend and professional comic artist named Matt Waite, but he wasn't a regular on the project. If I were pitching this graphic novel to a publishing company as a first-time creator, I wouldn't have even gotten the courtesy of a rejection letter. Yet on Kickstarter, my project was funded. With a great video, great graphics, a strong audience, and a robust marketing plan to be sure. But ultimately, it's all smoke and mirrors.

The thought of what I could have raised with more completed product keeps me up at night, truly. There's no substitute for a free sample, so imagine if folks could have read, say, a five-page excerpt from the book? They go from knowing nothing about a product they've never heard of to maybe getting engrossed into my story. As the saying goes, the proof of the pudding is in the eating.

I'm taking this advice on my next campaign. The next campaign I'm managing is for a space-themed card game called "Cosmonauts." With Cosmonauts, we already have a print-and-play version, and the only thing that's *not* completed is all the artwork for each of the game's 96 cards. But the campaign won't launch until ALL of the artwork is complete.

What's more, we've created a print-and-play version for two purposes: first, to send to reviewers and second, to play-test. Play-testing helps us grow our audience by getting people invested in the game's creation, as well as give us genuine feedback about the creation of the game and its fun value.

If you don't have enough of your product to show off, people may not get a sense of how awesome and unique it's going to be. But that's the best case scenario. The worst case scenario is that they get the WRONG idea of what your product is.

A CAUTIONARY TALE

There's a lot to learn from the infamous Kickstarter project *Zano*[9], "the world's most sophisticated nano drone,"

---

[9] https://www.kickstarter.com/projects/torquing/zano-autonomous-intelligent-swarming-nano-drone/description

but we're going to be using this ill-fated project to show how important expectations are - for your backers, and for you.

The Zano was advertised as a flying drone that could fit in the palm of your hand. The truly spectacular Kickstarter video boasted the ability to take aerial photos and HD video, hover or follow the user, and even be remote controlled via smartphone. The Zano fleet would be networked to servers constantly feeding new firmware and features so the Zano would remain developable long after competitors became obsolete. The problem is, when the campaign launched, Zano couldn't do any of these things.

It's difficult to know exactly how far along the product was when they launched the campaign, but later reports revealed that Zano could never do exactly what was promised. Accusations flew about CGI enhancements to the Kickstarter video to simulate Zano's most spectacular features. Kickstarter even updated its rules to prohibit exactly that:

> "When a project involves manufacturing and distributing something complex, like a gadget, we require projects to show backers a prototype of what they're making, and we prohibit photorealistic renderings."[10]

----

[10] Kickstarter. "Our Rules." https://www.kickstarter.com/rules?ref=footer

As of this writing, Kickstarter does not require you to show *them* a working prototype, but you'd better have one. And Kickstarter has integrity specialists on staff whose job it is to look for questionable projects and investigate their claims.

Much has been written about Zano, and we may never know the full story, but this much seems clear: the project was not a scam. Or at least, it wasn't intended to be. The developers fully expected to build the project they were promising. What's also clear is that they were never able to follow through on those promises, because of the 12,000 plus backers and the uncertain number of preorders, only four people ever received Zanos, and none of them worked properly. [11]

The moral of the story is, because the project creators (the Torquing Group Ltd) had unrealistic expectations of what they could accomplish, and because backers bought into those expectations (literally), this project failed - despite raising over $3 million U.S. dollars. And if you still don't think that's a failure, consider that the Torquing Group is bankrupt, and none of the backers will be receiving their rewards.

This problem could have been avoided if the project had been further along before launching a Kickstarter

---

[11] Harris, Mark. "How Zano Raised Millions on Kickstarter and Left Most Backers with Nothing - Kickstarter." Medium. 18 Jan. 2016. Web. https://medium.com/kickstarter/how-zano-raised-millions-on-kickstarter-and-left-backers-with-nearly-nothing-85c0abe4a6cb#.jj4ydqani

campaign. Should Zano have worked perfectly? Maybe not, but its basic features should have been completed even if every bell and whistle wasn't 100%. Should your project be complete before you launch? How far along *should* it be?

MVP

Successful product development - and crowdfunding - depends on you identifying your minimum viable product. A minimum viable product (MVP) is the simplest version of what you want to make that still retains that special something that sets you apart.

Tyler James, a crowdfunding practitioner/comic book publisher/podcaster, likes to call it a "minimum lovable product." Tyler's description hits the nail on the head:

> "Kickstarter is about passion. It's about putting out products that you would love to make, and love to bring into the world, and that your backers are going to love. So when you're thinking about your [minimum lovable product] you're thinking about what's the least you can do where you and your audience are going to be thrilled about your project."[12]

Let's use a few examples. If you're making a board game, does it need metal dice or plastic figurines? Those can

---

[12] James, Tyler. "5 Things You MUST Do Before Launching A Kickstarter Campaign." Podcast comment. ComixLaunch. 16 Aug. 2015. Web. http://www.comixlaunch.com/005/

both be stretch goals, and your game could still be awesome with regular dice and cardboard pogs in the meantime. If you're writing a book, does it need to be in leather-bound, foil-embossed hardcover? Or should that be a stretch goal (that actually sounds like three stretch goals to me, but what do I know?).

This is particularly important if you're adding nonessential features that are - shall we call them - experimental. So if you're making, say, a flying drone, maybe the heavy-duty casing that throws off the thing's weight and forces you into a total redesign of the motor is a deluxe design feature you should wait on.

The MVP is essential for the budgeting phase as you figure out your Kickstarter goal. This is because it's better to hit a lower goal and struggle for stretch goals than struggle to meet your original goal because you're trying to fund the deluxe version of your product. But I bring this up here instead because I believe you should be able to physically create your MVP (or already have created it) by the time you launch your campaign.

Do you remember when we talked about the Coolest Cooler? The highest-funded Kickstarter of all time that still hasn't fulfilled its rewards? Since the project was funded, the creators have shared over 30 updates about the continuing development of the product and the myriad production delays. The project not only had serious cashflow problems from failure to budget, but the design also changed several times, always with unintended consequences. As one

Coolest Cooler backer told me, "I would have been happy with the product in its original form if I could have it by now."

It's far from the only problem with the Coolest Cooler, but if the creators had stuck to their original MVP, they might have been able to avoid some of these fatal cashflow problems.

Which is why I urge you that whatever it is you're making, be able to make it. This is especially important with technology projects or consumer products, where production/manufacturing/design is a real concern. This is less serious with books or art, but then again, maybe it's not such a given. So whatever it is you want to make, be damn sure you can make it.

PUT UP OR SHUT UP

Another important reason to make sure your project is well on its way by the time you launch your campaign is to show the backers you're serious. They don't just want to know that you *can* do it - they want to know that you care about it.

Yes, to a certain extent, crowdfunding is the chance to see if the market wants your product before you invest your valuable resources into creating it. But, at the same time, if you don't care enough about your product to invest some of your resources into it now, why should anyone else?

Tyler James calls it "putting some skin in the game." As he puts it:

> "The campaign should not be a prerequisite for getting started on your product...understand that the more you complete of your project before crowdfunding it, the less risk there is that the project will never get finished. And that's less risk for you, and less risk for your backers."[13]

The bottom line is this: the more of your product is done, the more you audience can get an accurate feel for it - enticing new backers, and managing everyone's expectations. The more of your project that's done, the more your passion and belief will pass on to your backers. And the more confident they will feel that you can create the MVP you promised them.

That's why I suggest that you define your MVP, and make it as simple as possible while still being awesome so you can be sure that you can deliver the goods come fulfillment time.

---

[13] Ibid

CHAPTER 6

YOU HAVEN'T PLANNED FOR FULFILLMENT

It's fulfillment time. You ran your Kickstarter, made a bunch of money, and made your product. Everything went according to plan. But now you're trying to pack and ship dozens - or hundreds - of rewards. Keeping the pledge levels straight is hard enough, let alone backer's information. Then there's that one backer who changed their address after your Kickstarter survey - who was that again? Oh yeah, and there's that one backer you promised that thing to. You remember that thing, right? And then there's your mom and your cat, and they both said you didn't have to ship to them because they'd be happy to come pick it up from you. That saves a bit of money until - uh-oh, spaghetti-ohs! You're out of money because international shipping is REALLY expensive. Who knew?

You should have. And that's why your Kickstarter project is going to fail, even though it got funded - because you didn't plan for fulfillment.

Fortunately, it's not too late for that either. Fulfillment runs through a couple of the themes we've touched on so far, so we're going to go back to the beginning to see how you should be considering fulfillment at each stage of the game.

No Accounting For Taste

Understand this: your Kickstarter goal INCLUDES any money for shipping/handling. You don't get your goal PLUS shipping - so you have to price it in.

So if your product is going to cost $5,000 to make, that's not your goal (we've already discussed the Kickstarter cut and credit card processing fees). Your goal is $5,000 PLUS whatever it's going to cost to ship those rewards to your backers.

Well, how are you supposed to know how many backers you're going to have *before* you launch? Short answer: you guess. Don't worry, guessing is hard, I'll help you.

Remember that the average Kickstarter pledge is $25. So we can come up with a guesstimate of how many backers your project will have (if it's to be successful) by taking your goal and dividing by $25. So in my example, $5,000 divided by $25 is 200 backers.

So now you need to take your product and figure out what it costs to ship to those backers. How do you do that?

Pack it up, and weigh it. Seriously. Then you can plug that weight into the website of your common carrier of choice - UPS, DHL, whatever - and calculate shipping.

DO'S AND DON'TS

When you calculate your costs for shipping, **do**:

- calculate shipping for addresses in different parts of the United States;
- calculate international shipping to countries around the world (if you want to offer international shipping); and
- take into account the cost of boxes/packing material.

And when you're preparing to pack and ship your rewards, **don't**:

- underestimate anything - better to have more money than not enough;
- weigh your rewards for shipment until you've packed them the way you intend to send them; or
- forget to price match different carriers to get the best rate.

DIGITIZE ME, CAP'N!

"That's great, you dinosaur," you say to me with the aggressive tone I've come to expect from you. "But it's the 21st century and my product is *all* digital. So I don't need to worry about shipping!"

Slow clap, my friend, well done. But how will you distribute your digital rewards?

You could e-mail your reward, sure - and if it's a low-res PDF, as in a graphic novel or a book, that *might* work - if the attachment isn't too large. A graphic novel is pushing it - what if you're distributing music or film? E-mail is most certainly not going to work.

But there are easy, cheap options to share these large files. You can get really fancy and store them on a remote server, then provide your backers password access to that server to download the file. If this sounds complicated, it's because it probably is. But there are services now that give you similar functionality for low or no cost.

Dropbox, Google, and Amazon all have cloud-storage services for your documents, which allow you to share access with collaborators AND control their level of access. With Dropbox, for instance, you can upload your reward then share a download link via e-mail. What's more, basic access if FREE. And, you can use this for project collaboration, document sharing, and storage, so if you do have to pay for one of these services you can get a lot of bang for your buck.

ONE AND DONE

Now that you know how you plan to ship or otherwise deliver your rewards, you need a lot of information to distribute that information correctly. Think about it - you need names and addresses, sure, but what else do you need to know?

Did you promise a t-shirt? Then you need the size. Did you promise an inscription? You need the copy. You get the idea.

Fortunately, you don't have to e-mail every backer individually and combine the info into a spreadsheet - you can use the Kickstarter survey, which you already know because you backed some Kickstarter projects way back in chapter two. *Glares suspiciously*

Kickstarter allows you to run a survey to collect the information you need, where you can ask almost anything you want, including multiple choice questions. What you do with the answers is up to you.

But the Kickstarter survey is EXTREMELY limited in an important way - you only get one of them. If you forget to ask a question, you have to contact everyone manually to collect the information. If someone needs to update their information, like a change of address, they *can* do it through Kickstarter - but if they don't know that, they'll message you and YOU have to keep track manually. And certain things you can't do directly from the survey, like adding people to your e-mail list, need to be done separately.

So plan your survey out in advance, before your campaign ends. People are going to expect to see that survey within 24-48 hours of the end of your campaign or they'll think you're sleeping on the job.

Scaling Up

If you're going to have anywhere between 1 and 100 backers, chances are you can probably pack everything up to ship yourself. It could take some time, but with a little help from your friends, you can probably get it all done in a few hours if you really put your nose to the grindstone.

But once you're talking about more than 100 backers, probably with at least a dozen different rewards levels, things are going to get *very* time-consuming and *very* complicated. And if your backers begin to number into the thousands, you WILL need professional help.

There are companies who specialize in fulfillment, who can offer you storage, packing, and shipping - for a price of course. You can even have Amazon fulfill your rewards, which is very efficient if you plan to sell your product on Amazon anyway and planned to let them fulfill your orders. And there are companies who specialize in data management, who can keep track of your backers and their rewards and convey that information in a meaningful way to a fulfillment company.

You might be thinking, you can't possibly afford these services. On that note, I disagree for two reasons. First, because you can price such costs into your Kickstarter goal (if you have a reasonable guess of how many backers you're going to have). Second, how can you afford *not* to use these services? Your time is worth something - even at minimum wage, the time it would take to fulfill thousands of backer rewards is astronomical. And your time is better spent creating your product and marketing it to people. So don't waste your time - and thereby, your money - by taking on the headache of a huge fulfillment project like this one.

Trust the experts.

CHAPTER 7

WHAT'S NEXT

Like we talked about at the beginning, this book is not about running a successful Kickstarter campaign. It IS about avoiding certain failure.

If you want to run a truly gangbusters Kickstarter campaign, you're on the right track. Reading this book means you're already looking for resources, gathering information, and planning your course of action.

ADDITIONAL RESOURCES

You should continue to do your research. The world is full of wisdom on crowdfunding in podcasts, webinars, blogs, books, and more. This book is my humble contribution to the collective consciousness I turned to when creating my campaign. I have a few parting offers to make you as you set out on your journey to crowdfunding success.

On www.carmelochimera.com, you can sign up for my e-mail list where I will send a FREE weekly newsletter filled with practical advice for entrepreneurs, covering topics like crowdfunding, audience building, work-life balance and more. I'll also let you know about upcoming workshops and webinars. And, I'll share a link to my new weekly podcast, Chimera Solutions. Chimera Solutions provides inspiration, information, and innovation to entrepreneurs in 20 minutes or less. On this podcast, I'll share my experiences, interview entrepreneurs, and review books that will help you make your wildest dreams come true.

If you found this book at all valuable, I promise you there's a LOT more where that came from.

ASK CARMELO

When it comes to doing research, I'm fond of quoting *Burn Notice*'s main character, Michael Weston: "There's no substitute for human intelligence."

All the books, blogs, and podcasts in the world are no substitute for a live human being you can talk to. If you need my help, I'd be happy to provide whatever you need - from a few short planning sessions to answer questions and brainstorm ideas, all the way to managing your entire campaign. I also provide coaching and consultation, as well as legal services, to businesses.

You can contact me at www.carmelochimera.com today, and we'll figure out what works best for you.

NEXT TIME

While this book is not about Kickstarter success, my *next* book is. Coming soon, *The ABC's of Kickstarter: A Beginner's Guide To Crowdfunding* will share ALL of the knowledge and research I've accumulated over the past year. I spent countless hours and sleepless nights gathering cross-disciplinary research to make sure I succeeded at Kickstarter *on the first try*. This book will take you by the hand through each area of crowdfunding, incorporating philosophy, psychology, behavioral economics, and more to show you the tried-and-true path to crowdfunding success. Sign up for my mailing list to find out when this book will be available, or preorder now on Amazon.

CONTACT ME

There's a few ways to reach me to discuss the topics in this book, suggest corrections or revisions, or discuss your crowdfunding or business needs:

- **On The Web:** www.carmelochimera.com
- **LinkedIn:** http://bit.ly/1s8OoO1

"No individual has sufficient experience, education, native ability, and knowledge to insure the accumulation of a great fortune, without the cooperation of other people."

Napoleon Hill